VOCAL SELECTIONS

I Love You, You're Perfect, Now Change

Dedicated to the memory of Jamie Hammerstein
producer, mentor and friend

ACKNOWLEDGEMENTS: Nicholas Levin, original music preparation;
Bill Grossman, proofreading; Tom Fay, original music direction; Joel Bishoff,
Jonathan Pollard and Bernie Kukoff for their invaluable support and guidance;
and original cast members: Robert Roznowski, Jennifer Simard, Melissa Weil,
Robert Michael Baker and Jordan Leeds.

Stock and Amateur rights for
I Love You, You're Perfect, Now Change
are licensed by The Rodgers & Hammerstein Theatre Library
Tel: 212/564-4000 // Fax 212/268-1245 // E-mail: theatre@rnh.com
www.rnh.com

ISBN 978-0-634-00933-4

WILLIAMSON MUSIC®
A RODGERS AND HAMMERSTEIN COMPANY
www.williamsonmusic.com

EXCLUSIVELY DISTRIBUTED BY

HAL•LEONARD®
CORPORATION
7777 W. BLUEMOUND RD. P.O. BOX 13819 MILWAUKEE, WI 53213

Visit Hal Leonard Online at
www.halleonard.com

WESTSIDE THEATRE
(UPSTAIRS)

JAMES HAMMERSTEIN BERNIE KUKOFF JONATHAN POLLARD

present

I LOVE YOU,
YOU'RE PERFECT,
NOW CHANGE

Book and Lyrics by
JOE DIPIETRO

Music by
JIMMY ROBERTS

with

JORDAN LEEDS
JENNIFER SIMARD

ROBERT ROZNOWSKI
MELISSA WEIL

Scenic Design
**NEIL PETER
JAMPOLIS**

Costume Design
**CANDICE
DONNELLY**

Lighting Design
**MARY LOUISE
GEIGER**

Sound Design
**DUNCAN
EDWARDS**

Production Supervisor
**MATTHEW G.
MARHOLIN**

Associate Producer
**MATT
GARFIELD**

*General
Management*
**ROBERT V. STRAUS
PRODUCTIONS**

*Press
Representative*
**BILL EVANS
& ASSOCIATES**

*Vocal & Instrumental
Arrangements*
**JIMMY
ROBERTS**

Musical Direction by
TOM FAY

Directed by
JOEL BISHOFF

Presented at The Long Wharf Theatre, Arvin Brown, Artistic Director, M. Edgar Rosenblum, Executive Director, May 9-June 9, 1996. Originally produced by The American Stage Company, James N. Vagias, Executive Producer.

Program from Opening Night, August 1, 1996, Westside Theatre, New York City

I Love You, You're Perfect, Now Change

A STUD AND A BABE

Lyrics by JOE DiPIETRO
Music by JIMMY ROBERTS

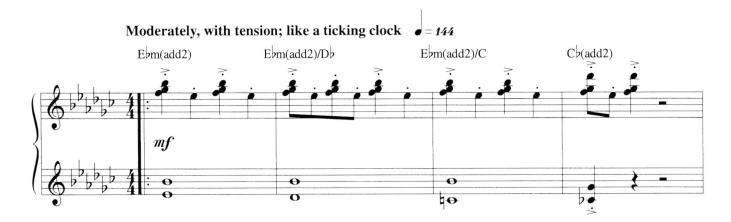

Moderately, with tension; like a ticking clock ♩ = 144

Jason: Did I mention I just had my phone fixed?
Julie: Really?
Jason: Yes.
Julie: Oh?
Jason: Yeah.
Julie: Wow.
Jason: Yeah.

(Wait a beat)

Julie: Oh, I just remembered the cutest story about my brother!
Jason: Oh, what?
Julie: No, maybe not...
Jason: No, c'mon, c'mon!
Julie: Okay, my brother - this is really cute -
Jason: Yeah, yeah, yeah?
Julie: He has eleven toes!

(Wait a beat)

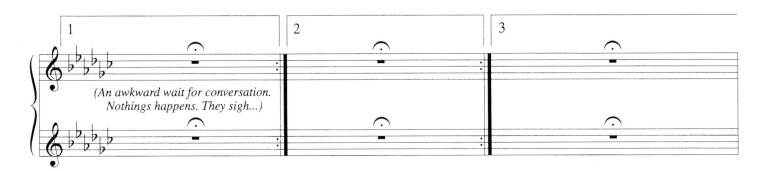

(An awkward wait for conversation. Nothings happens. They sigh...)

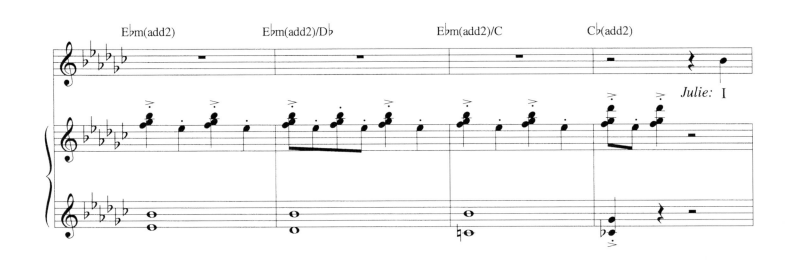

Julie: I

Faster, wilder, with a strong rock beat ♩ = *160*

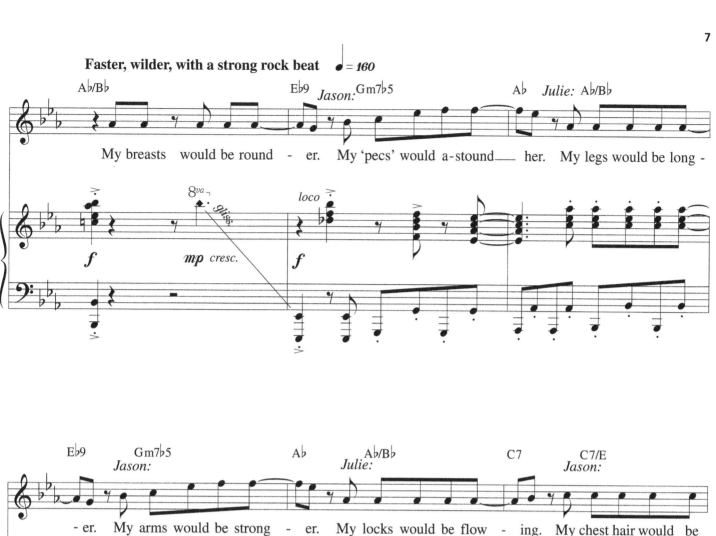

My breasts would be round - er. My 'pecs' would a-stound___ her. My legs would be long -

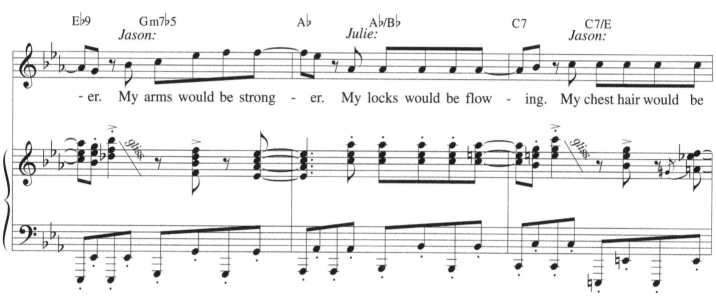

- er. My arms would be strong - er. My locks would be flow - ing. My chest hair would be

show - ing.___ My hips would be slim - mer. My butt would just sim - mer.

Tempo I

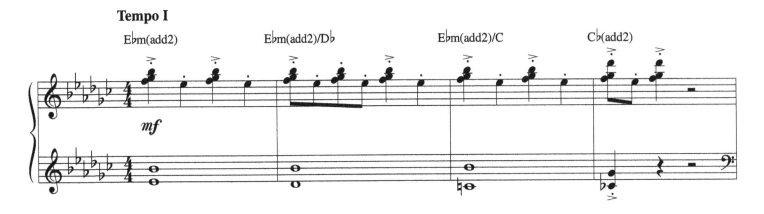

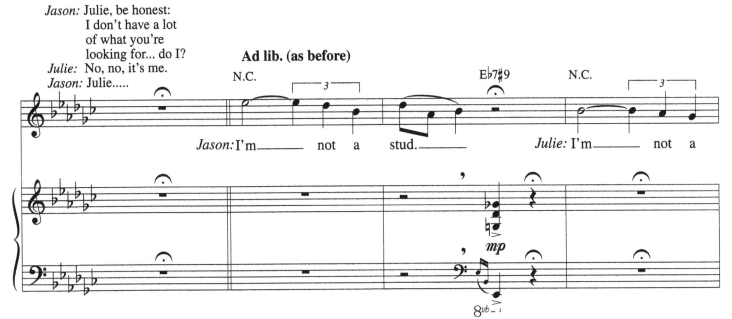

SINGLE MAN DROUGHT

Lyrics by JOE DiPIETRO
Music by JIMMY ROBERTS

him a - round,___ there's a se - ri - ous sin - gle man___ drought.

Veronica: I can't be - lieve he's talk - ing___ still.___

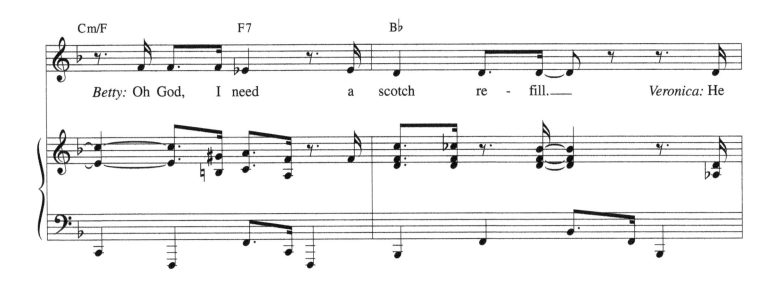

Betty: Oh God, I need a scotch re - fill.___ *Veronica:* He

18

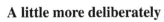

A little more deliberately

I date Bob, and hope, and flirt;

he might get bet - ter___ by des - sert.___ I

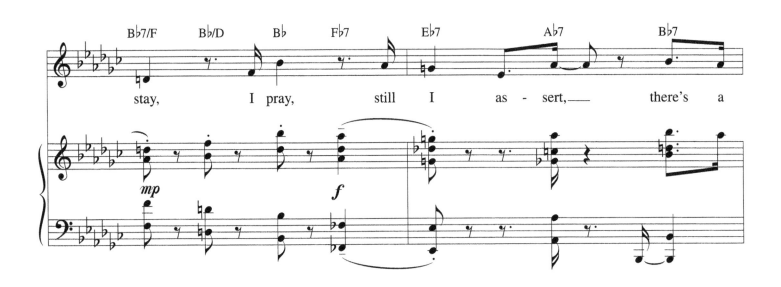

stay, I pray, still I as - sert,___ there's a

TEAR JERK

Lyrics by JOE DiPIETRO
Music by JIMMY ROBERTS

she goes: "Well, what mov-ie should we do?" So I go: "Well, that is

ful-ly up to you." And that, my friends, was my one big mis-

take.

My

mov - ie sat - is - fac - tion is mind - less vi - 'lent ac - tion; some

mus - cle men___ who tus - sle with___ Stal - lone. A

thril - la that___ would thrill us, with Ar - nold or___ Bruce Wil - lis, and

lots of na - ked shots of Sha - ron Stone. This

I WILL BE LOVED TONIGHT

Lyrics by JOE DiPIETRO
Music by JIMMY ROBERTS

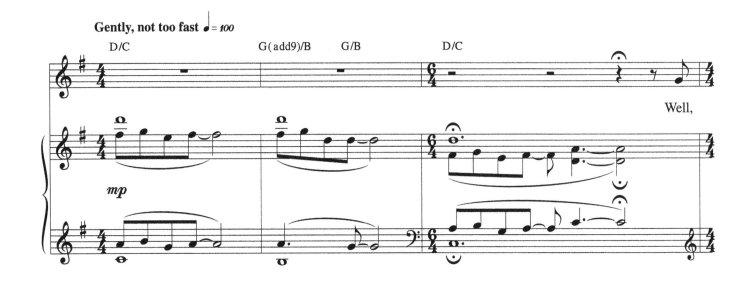

Gently, not too fast ♩ = 100

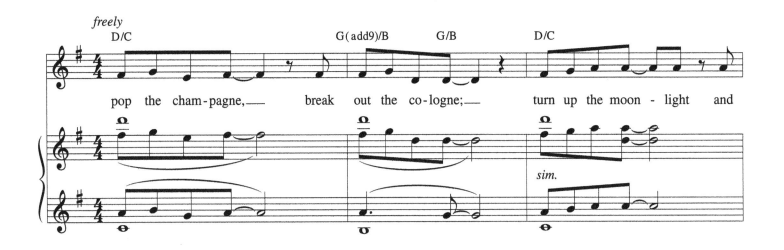

pop the cham-pagne,___ break out the co-logne;___ turn up the moon - light and

turn off the phone.___ Well, what a sur-prise,___ a man is in sight; and

ALWAYS A BRIDESMAID

Lyrics by JOE DiPIETRO
Music by JIMMY ROBERTS

42

THE BABY SONG

Lyrics by JOE DiPIETRO
Music by JIMMY ROBERTS

boo!

Now I hear my ba-by cry-cry; so it's time that I go bye-bye. Doo-ba, dab-by, dee-by, dub-by, wee-ba, woo-by, woo.

MARRIAGE TANGO

Lyrics by JOE DiPIETRO
Music by JIMMY ROBERTS

With a dramatic Tango feel ♩ = *120*

who would have guessed, but soon I'll be un-dressed; I'm

mar-ried, and I'm gon-na have sex!

Marlene: I laid out their school clothes, and the left-o-vers I froze, so I'm

SHOULDN'T I BE LESS IN LOVE WITH YOU?

Lyrics by JOE DiPIETRO
Music by JIMMY ROBERTS

* (Grace notes in measures 5 and 9 differ from previous grace notes)

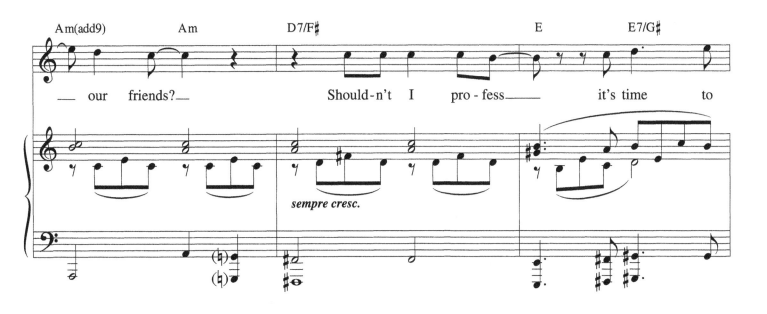

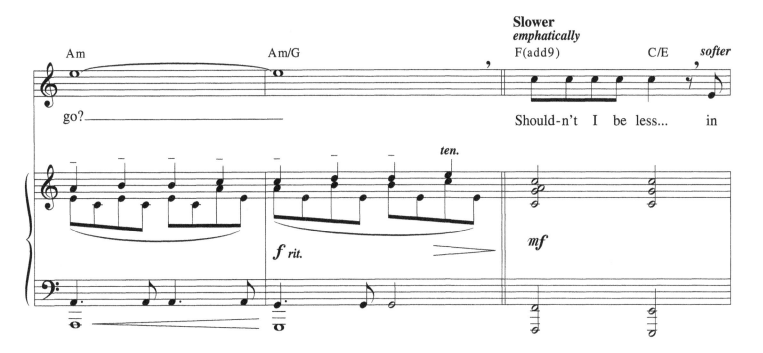

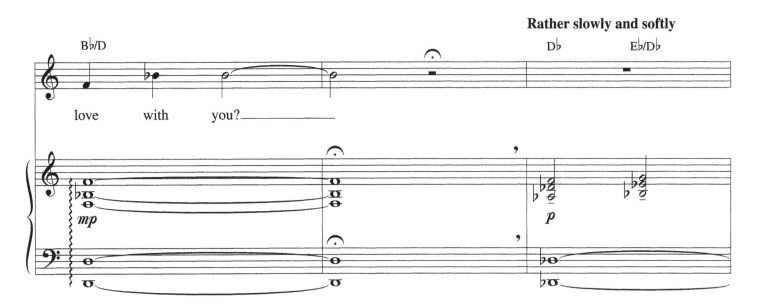

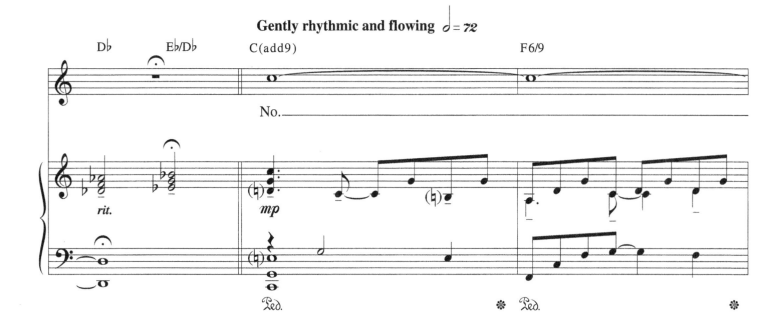

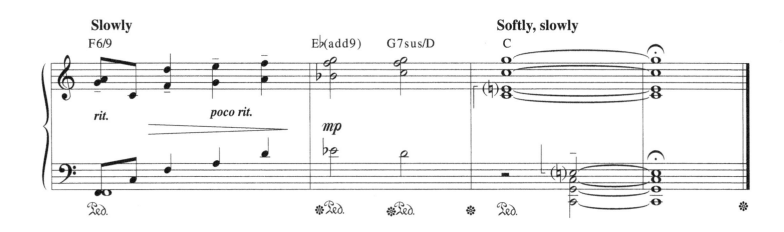

I CAN LIVE WITH THAT

Lyrics by JOE DiPIETRO
Music by JIMMY ROBERTS

70

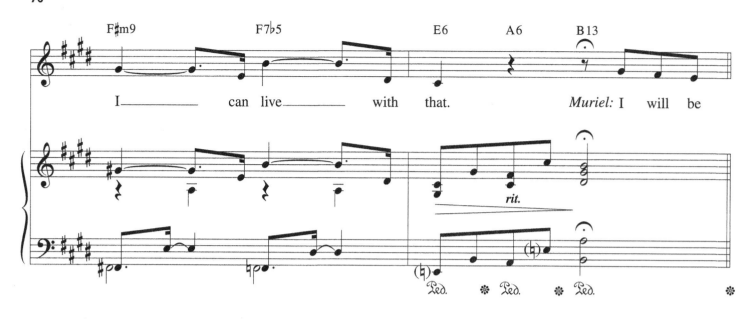

I_____ can live_____ with that. *Muriel:* I will be

Slowly, tenderly, rather freely ♩ = *84*

bur - ied at my Jim's right. *Arthur:* Next to my

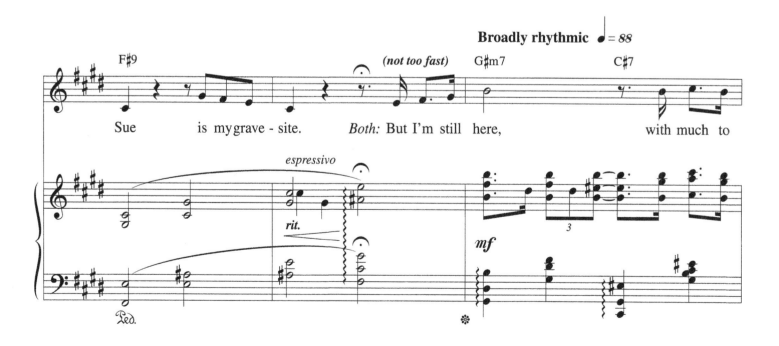

Broadly rhythmic ♩ = *88*

Sue is my grave - site. *Both:* But I'm still here, with much to

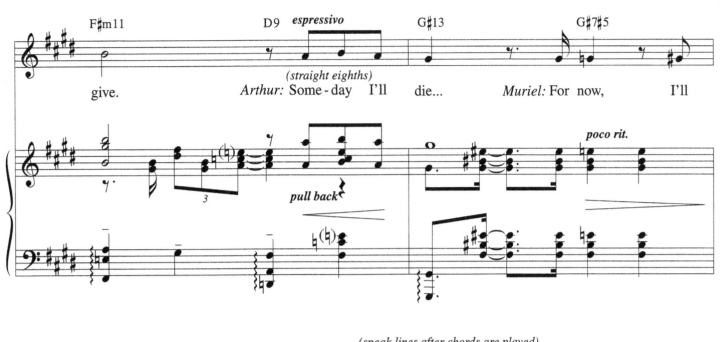

give. *Arthur:* Some-day I'll die... *Muriel:* For now, I'll

(straight eighths)

(speak lines after chords are played)

live. *Muriel:* "I'll always love my Jim." *Arthur:* "And I my Sue."

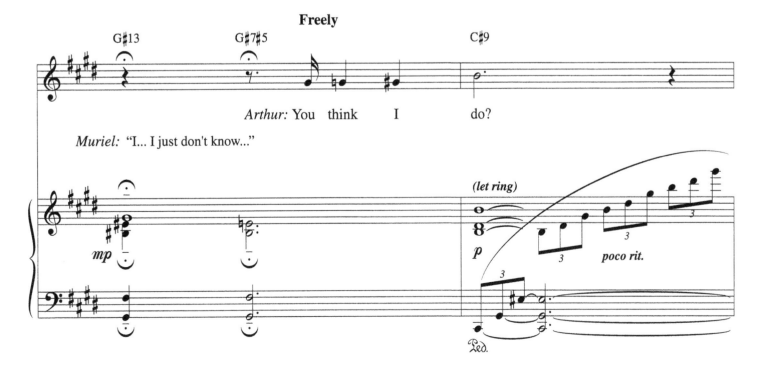

Freely

Arthur: You think I do?

Muriel: "I... I just don't know..."

I LOVE YOU, YOU'RE PERFECT, NOW CHANGE

(Finale)

Lyrics by JOE DiPIETRO
Music by JIMMY ROBERTS

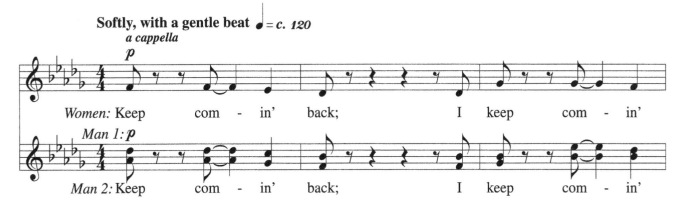

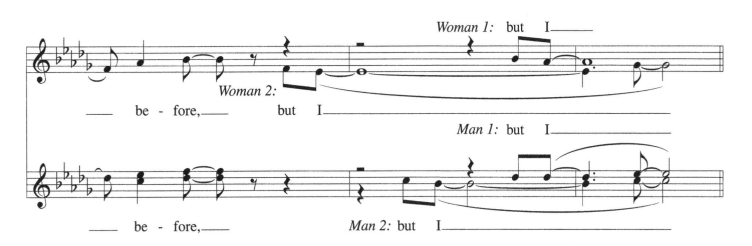